WE ARE ALL
FLOWERS

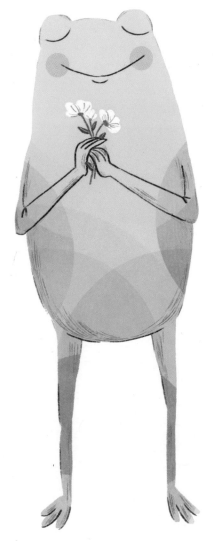

WE ARE ALL FLOWERS

BY **ORLAITH O'SULLIVAN**

ILLUSTRATED BY
TIKA AND TATA

PLUM BLOSSOM
BOOKS

BERKELEY, CALIFORNIA

PLUM BLOSSOM BOOKS

Plum Blossom Books, the children's imprint of Parallax Press, publishes books on mindfulness for young people and the grown-ups in their lives.

Parallax Press
2236B Sixth Street
Berkeley, California 94710
parallax.org

ISBN: 978–1–952692–13–0

Library of Congress Cataloging-in-Publication Data
Names: O'Sullivan, Orlaith, author. | Tika and Tata (Illustrator), illustrator.
Title: We are all flowers / words by Orlaith O'Sullivan ; illustrations by Tika and
   Tata.
Identifiers: LCCN 2021061307 (print) | LCCN 2021061308 (ebook) |
   ISBN 9781952692130 (hardcover) | ISBN 9781952692147 (ebook)
LC record available at https://lccn.loc.gov/2021061307
LC ebook record available at https://lccn.loc.gov/2021061308

Printed in Canada

1 2 3 4 5 / 26 25 24 23 22

To my mother, Pauline,
and my teacher Thich Nhat Hanh,
who taught me how to garden

We are all flowers,
each and every one,

We're freshened by water;
we reach towards the sun.

Sometimes we're strong flowers—superconfident,
Like a big dandelion pushing up through cement,

And some days we're droopy,
A bit tired or unsure,
A bit worried
or lonely
or sad
or heartsore.

We have droopy times, so it's just great to know,
How refreshing each other helps flowers to grow.

It helps you and your friends and your family and me,
And your classmates and teammates and community.

You can change the whole day if you
can water one flower,

You can change the whole world with . . .

SUPERWATERINGPOWER!

So how do we do it? Here's a pathway that's clear,
Three steps to success in your gardening career:

1.

Start from your heart.
It just has to be true.
No fake flower watering.
It has to be you.

2. Find someone you love; bring them into your heart,
Draw them in nice and close so they really take part.

You might notice their eyes or their smile or their voice
Or their hands or their laugh or their toes—it's your choice.

What do you feel with
this person so dear?

What things do you sense
when this person is near?

Snuggled or cared for,
loved or heartwarmed?

Included or just safe,
your worries transformed?

3. Now get superspecific. What on earth do they do

That you're happy they're them and so happy you're you?

It can be big or little, something loving or wise,
Or patient or generous or a lovely surprise.

It can be them *not* shouting when you were so cross,
Or making ice cream with the best chocolate sauce.

Maybe holding you close
when you were so scared,

Or listening deeply
so you felt really heard.

It can be anything, so let your heart explore
And find *one* thing about them that you just adore.

Don't fill up a bucket and drench them all quick,
A gentle cascade is what will do the trick.

With precision and care, you can refresh with ease,
And their hearts will blossom with your expertise.

When we water flowers,
we're presenting a prize,

And people can glimpse how
things look through our eyes.

We all see things differently; things mean different things.
Some of us love seesaws and some of us swings.

Some love bedtime songs;
they help us rest deep,

Some yank up the covers,
"I'm trying to *sleep*!"

Flower watering helps us
to be known and seen,

So we know how things feel
when they mean what they mean.

With practice, flower watering is an everyday joy,
It's indubitably a great skill to employ.
It helps everyone know that you know that they're there,
And you know that they're kind
And you know that they care.

So go forth, wise gardeners, and reenergize
All the beautiful flowers so dear to your eyes,
All the ways that they care for you, you recognize.

But wait! There's a *fourth* step
That's crucial to know,

For sometimes *you're* droopy,
No energy to grow.

There are goggles of gloominess we sometimes wear,
And we feel a bit rubbish, and it feels hard to care.

This is just when we muster our kindness and strength,
To help us retune to a better wavelength.

We remember small things that we did or we said:

We took care of our sleepy selves by going to bed,

We brushed teeth and we tidied, we offered to share,

We snuggled our pet so that they know we care,

We rested and played and we learned and explored,
We dreamed and we tried to be patient when bored,
We gave someone a hug or our words brought a smile,
We took care of our anger, which was so worthwhile:
Coming back to our body, feeling safe and at home,
Breathing deep in our belly, at peace in the zone.

There were times we helped loads with our kind open heart,
Drop by drop we remember, and you'll find once you start
That a giant cascade of heart-pouring pours out,

And you've more than you need now, without a doubt,
Filling up watering cans and a wide reservoir,
Reminding you you're . . .

AMAZING!

just as you are.

So don't let it whoosh past; each drop of memory
Brings superstrength anti-droopy energy.

And you'll know you're a wonder,
aware of all that you do;

You'll remember your goodness,
And you'll sense this is true:

THE IMPORTANTEST
FLOWER TO WATER